Legendary Warriors

KNIGHTS

by Adrienne Lee

Reading Consultant:
Barbara J. Fox
Professor Emerita
North Carolina State University

CAPSTONE PRESS
a capstone imprint

Blazers Books are published by Capstone Press,
1710 Roe Crest Drive, North Mankato, Minnesota 56003
www.capstonepub.com

Library of Congress Cataloging-in-Publication Data
Cataloging-in-publication information is on file with the Library of Congress.
ISBN 978-1-4765-3115-1 (hardcover)
ISBN 978-1-4765-3373-5 (ebook PDF)

Editorial Credits
Megan Peterson and Mandy Robbins, editors; Kyle Grenz, designer; Wanda Winch, media
researcher; Jennifer Walker, production specialist

Photo Credits
Alamy: Lordprice Collection, 10; The Bridgeman Art Library: © Look and Learn/Private
Collection/Peter Jackson, 13, The Stapleton Collection/Private Collection/Walter Crane, 9;
Newscom: akg-images, 26; North Wind Picture Archives, 22-23, 25; Shutterstock: Algol, 23
(right), Antonio Abrignani, 8, bigredlynx, back cover (sword), boykov, 29, dtopal, 5 (knight),
javarman, cover (castle), Lenar Musin, 5 (castle), michelaubryphoto, 21 (bottom), Nejron
Photo, cover (knight), 19, 20, Olga Rutko, 16-17, Russell Shively, cover, 1 (b), Stocksnapper, 28;
SuperStock Inc: Fine Art Images, 14, SuperStock, 6

Printed in the United States of America in Stevens Point, Wisconsin.
032013   007227WZF13

Table of Contents

THE AGE OF KNIGHTHOOD

Long ago, knights thundered into battle on horseback. These deadly warriors fought for lords in Europe. Lords struggled to keep control of their land.

In the Middle Ages (AD 500-1500), Europe was made up of about 15 kingdoms. Each kingdom was made up of parts controlled by lords.

Being a knight cost a lot of money. Knights had to buy their own horses, weapons, and armor. Poor **peasants** could not afford to be knights. Most knights came from rich families.

IT'S A FACT

A warhorse was a knight's most expensive piece of equipment. A good horse cost more than most people earned in a lifetime.

peasant—a poor person who owns a small farm, especially in Europe and some Asian countries

Knights lived by a set of rules called **chivalry**. According to these rules, knights had to protect **Christians**. They also had to be honest and polite to women.

chivalry—a code of noble and polite behavior that was expected of a medieval knight
Christian—a person who follows a religion based on the teachings of Jesus

Knights rode into battle whenever one kingdom attacked another. They protected their lords' land. They also captured and defended castles.

Knights fought in the Crusades. They traveled to faraway countries to win lands controlled by non-Christians.

Crusades—battles fought between AD 1000 and 1300 by European Christians trying to capture lands from non-Christians

THE LIFE OF A KNIGHT

Training for knighthood began early. At age 7, the son of a knight or **nobleman** served as a page. Pages learned how to obey orders. A page became a **squire** around age 14.

nobleman—a wealthy person of high rank
squire—a young nobleman who helped a knight

IT'S A FACT

Squires trained with weapons and horses for four years. They also cared for knights' horses and weapons.

13

Most squires became knights through a ceremony called "dubbing." A squire swore an **oath** to serve his lord. Then a king, queen, or another knight tapped his shoulders with a sword. At that moment, a squire became a knight.

In rare cases, a squire might be called into battle. If he fought bravely, a squire could become a knight on the battlefield.

oath—a serious promise

Knights sometimes fought at contests called **tournaments**. Jousting was a popular event. In jousting, knights rode toward each other and tried to knock each other off their horses with spears.

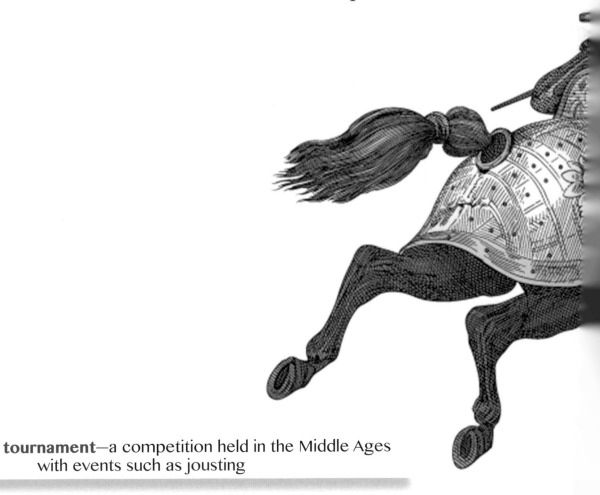

tournament—a competition held in the Middle Ages with events such as jousting

Many knights were killed during the first tournaments. Later special tournament spears were made. They had wooden tips that were safer to use.

A KNIGHT'S NECESSITIES

All knights wore armor. Early knights wore **chain mail** shirts. Later some knights wore suits of armor. A metal-plated suit covered a knight's entire body.

IT'S A FACT

Suits of armor often weighed more than 50 pounds (23 kilograms). They were so heavy that some knights needed help climbing onto their horses.

chain mail—armor made up of thousands of tiny iron rings linked together

chain mail

A sword was a knight's most important weapon. The longsword and greatsword were heavy enough to split armor. A greatsword weighed as much as 20 pounds (9 kg).

↓ **greatsword**

Knights rode side by side, crushing enemy foot soldiers in their path. Together, each horse and knight weighed nearly 2,000 pounds (900 kg).

If a knight fell from his horse during battle, he was in great danger. His heavy armor slowed him down.

↑ a knight holding a polearm

THE END OF AN AGE

Knighthood began to fade in the 1400s and 1500s. Guns and cannons were common on European battlefields by the late 1400s. Knights were no match for the power of guns.

an illustration of English soldiers pulling in a cannon to attack a French castle in 1347 ➡

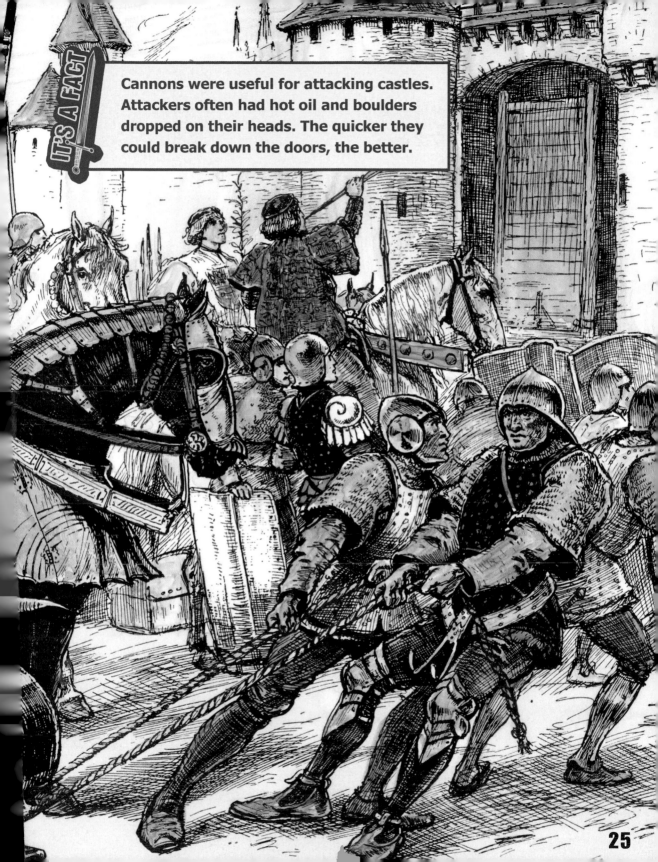

Cannons were useful for attacking castles. Attackers often had hot oil and boulders dropped on their heads. The quicker they could break down the doors, the better.

 Swiss mercenaries at the Battle of Marignano in 1515

In 1494 a group of Italy's finest knights attacked French soldiers. The French soldiers killed the knights with musket balls fired from guns.

The cost of keeping knights was high. Kings rewarded knights with land and money. But kings only had so much to give. They began hiring Swiss and German **mercenaries**. By the 1500s, knights were no longer used in battles.

mercenary—a soldier who is paid to fight for a foreign army

The lives of the knights continue to interest people today. Jousting contests are still held around the world. Knights often appear in books and movies. They live on as symbols of courage and honor.

GLOSSARY

chain mail (CHAYN MAYL)—armor made up of thousands of tiny iron rings linked together

chivalry (SHIV-uhl-ree)—a code of noble and polite behavior that was expected of a medieval knight

Christian (KRIS-chuhn)—a person who follows a religion based on the teachings of Jesus

Crusades (kroo-SAYDZ)—battles fought between AD 1000 and 1300 by European Christians trying to capture lands from non-Christians

mercenary (MUR-suh-nayr-ee)—a soldier who is paid to fight for a foreign army

nobleman (NOH-buhl-muhn)—a wealthy person of high rank

oath (OHTH)—a serious promise

peasant (PEZ-uhnt)—a poor person who owns a small farm, especially in Europe and some Asian countries

squire (SKWIRE)—a young nobleman who helped a knight

tournament (TUR-nuh-muhnt)—a competition held in the Middle Ages with events such as jousting

READ MORE

Guillain, Charlotte. *Medieval Knights.* Fierce Fighters. Chicago: Raintree, 2010.

Mason, Paul. *Want to Be a Knight?* Crabtree Connections. New York: Crabtree Pub. Co., 2012.

Stiefel, Chana. *Sweaty Suits of Armor: Could You Survive Being a Knight?* Ye Yucky Middle Ages. Berkeley Heights, N.J.: Enslow Publishers, 2012.

INTERNET SITES

FactHound offers a safe, fun way to find Internet sites related to this book. All of the sites on FactHound have been researched by our staff.

Here's all you do:

Visit *www.facthound.com*

Type in this code: 9781476531151

Check out projects, games and lots more at
www.capstonekids.com

INDEX